GRACE
and
GRATITUDE

What a wonderful title: Grace and Gratitude.

This book is a gift to the reader as Brian Gallagher writes naturally in his easy, encouraging, friendly manner. The chapter headings form a structure that keeps God's gift first and foremost and leads to trust in this gifting God.

A creative feature is the inclusion of music and song that entice deep feeling from the heart. The deeper feeling is conveyed by reference to Olivia Newton-John's song "Grace and Gratitude" which provides the title for the book and the positive outlook of Louis Armstrong's "It's a wonderful world". Life in death gives us The Last Post and "The Band played Waltzing Matilda". The powerful Mahler Resurrection symphony is also drawn upon for deeper contemplation of life and death. Strong recommendation is given to the contemplative way of the awareness examen.

This book is an excellent reference for all searching to recognise and live with the gift of grace and gratitude in today's troubled world. Reading this book is a grace in itself.

Therese Quinn rsj
Artist and Spiritual Director

This excellent little book by Brian Gallagher offers a confident invitation to Hope. Distinct from optimism, which is a human attitude that can often be frustrated, Hope is a God-given virtue, much needed today when we hear of all the horrible things that we humans are inflicting upon one another and upon the planet we share with the rest of creation. Brian challenges us to keep trusting that the infinitely gracious and loving God is constantly at work, guiding us to the life-giving encounter that awaits us ultimately in death. In the world of war and climate change and in the inner world of our prayer life that often seems empty when nothing seems to be happening, we are invited again and again to be confident that God who loves us so tenderly is still at work within us.

Paul Castley msc
Spiritual Guide and Ministry Supervisor

In this telling of his personal experience of God, Brian Gallagher provides insights that entice us into the deepening places of our heart. We find wisdom in his words as he invites us into his vulnerabilities, and in doing this we perceive our own vulnerabilities and brokenness. He seeks to help us see beyond our senses to a deeper awareness of God's presence. Admitting to an emptiness, an aloneness, that is the very core of who he is. He describes it as "a deeper place inside me that no other person ever touches". He defines this as "a very precious place, a place to treasure and care for... a place of God". He speaks of his experiences of sitting in the apparent emptiness of prayer, something many readers will identify with. From this darkness emerges God's gifts of growth in inner freedom and truth. We are called to live God's heart, love and compassion as witnesses to God's love in us. God's gift to us is love and Brian's response to this is an ever-growing life of Grace and Gratitude. I would recommend this book to be read thoughtfully and prayerfully for all seeking deeper spirituality.

Anne Marmion
Chair, Parish Pastoral Council, Blackburn

Other Books of Brian Gallagher
published by Coventry Press

Communal Wisdom
Set Me Free
The Eyes of God
God's Foolishness
No Greater Love
The Joy of Ageing

GRACE and GRATITUDE

A way of life

BRIAN GALLAGHER MSC

COVENTRY PRESS

Published in Australia by
Coventry Press
33 Scoresby Road
Bayswater VIC 3153

ISBN 9781922589330

Copyright © Brian Gallagher msc 2023

All rights reserved. Other than for the purposes and subject to the conditions prescribed under the *Copyright Act*, no part of this publication may be reproduced, stored in a retrieval system, or transmitted in any form or by any means, electronic, mechanical, photocopying, recording or otherwise, without the prior permission of the publisher.

Scripture quotations are from the *New Revised Standard Version Bible*, copyright 1989, Division of Christian Education of the National Council of the Churches of Christ in the United States of America. Used by permission. All rights reserved.

Catalogue-in-Publication entry is available from the National Library of Australia http://catalogue.nla.gov.au

Cover design by Ian James – www.jgd.com.au
Text design by Coventry Press
Set in EB Garamond

Printed in Australia

Table of Contents

Introduction	9
Chapter One God's gifts	13
Chapter Two Living in gratitude	20
Chapter Three But...	29
Chapter Four Life in Death	38
Chapter Five Resurrection	45
Chapter Six Trust in God	51
Epilogue	56

Introduction

Mary MacKillop once said that 'gratitude is the memory of the heart'. The memories in my heart are overflowing. I marvel as I look back over my 60 years as a Missionary of the Sacred Heart (MSC). Fifty-five of those years have been in priestly ministry, thirty of them at Heart of Life Centre for Spiritual and Pastoral Formation (which I began in 1983), and twenty years living in Shoreham (where I set up a retreat centre that is still flourishing). Somewhere in there, I squeezed in six happy years at the leader of the MSC Australian province.

In all of those years, I have rejoiced in a ministry of supporting, caring for, guiding other people. Mary MacKillop is right: my uppermost sentiment is gratitude – not only because of such rich opportunities that have come my way, but more because I am well aware that they all came as gift. The Scripture text that has sustained me through those years is 'I know the one in whom I have put my trust' (2 Timothy 1:12). And that 'one' has blessed me abundantly.

In my early years as a priest, I was occasionally invited to give what was called a preached retreat. This involved a couple of daily talks on relevant topics to a group of any number from 5 to 50. I would not have had much personal contact with the retreatants, but I watched their faces closely as I sat there offering my thoughts and suggestions. On one occasion – it may even have been my first retreat – on the last day, the sister in charge of the community told me in no uncertain terms that I had been way too encouraging to the sisters.[1]

I didn't need to ask what she had been expecting. Her approach – maybe the norm at the time – would have been to stress keeping the rule, self-discipline, even self-denial. Some of those early emphases and practices in living a Christian life doubtless have a place. But I still cannot see them as primary. I still react to homilies that are too negative, too critical, too demanding on people. I still see myself wanting to encourage before all else.

I believe that we have every reason to be positive, hopeful, joyful in living our lives. Judging even by the titles of his publications, Pope Francis agrees. Though it seems to have been overlooked for years, I believe that the tradition in spirituality also agrees.

For example, in writing of her revelations in late fourteenth century, Julian of Norwich's constant theme was 'all will be well.' Her assurance that God had all things in hand led to her belief that the church had over-emphasised sin and damnation, at the expense of

---

1 In this and another story from my ministry in the first chapter, all details of time, place and circumstance have been sufficiently altered to make any recognition highly unlikely.

forgiveness and salvation. We may well sin, but like a child who has made a mistake, we turn to our loving parent – we turn to God who does not scold us, but embraces us lovingly.

> The greatest honour we can give Almighty God is
> to live gladly because of the knowledge of his love.[2]

Another example is found in St Francis de Sales, whom I have mentioned elsewhere in my writing. Francis was a popular bishop in France in the sixteenth century. He wrote two books in his life-time. The first he called An *Introduction to the Devout Life*, in which he focused on practices and habits Christian people need to cultivate to live a 'devout life': acts of charity, penance, ways of prayer, confession, etc. The second book, nine years later, focused rather on God's love for us and the ways God shows that love in our lives: A *Treatise on the Love of God*, this time focusing on God's gift not our effort to live well.[3]

Francis saw God's intimate personal love for each of us as foundational. From the moment of creation, God gives Godself to us in love:

> God's love has been poured into our hearts
> through the Holy Spirit that has been given to us.
> Romans 5:5

---

[2] Julian of Norwich, *Julian of Norwich: Showings* (Mahwah, N.J.:Paulist Press, 1977).
[3] Francis de Sales, *Treatise on the Love of God* (New York: Doubleday & Co, 1963).

God is loving self-giving. Nothing we do will change God's love for us. I have been blessed in my life to find God's loving care never far from my awareness. The way we live our lives lovingly, generously and gratefully is our response to this great gift of God. Olivia Newton-John's song *Grace and Gratitude* captures my theme beautifully. I develop that in what follows.

Chapter One

God's gifts

In another of her revelations, Julian of Norwich wrote:

> No created being can ever know how much
> and how sweetly and tenderly God loves them.[4]

There is no greater love, no greater gift. Many passages from the Scriptures affirm this:

> When I look to the heavens, the work of your fingers,
> the moon and the stars that you have established,
> What are human beings that you are mindful of them,
> mortals that you care for them?
> Yet you have made them a little lower than God.
> Psalm 8:3-5

As 'little less than God', we are God's chosen ones, deeply loved:

> I have called you by name, you are mine.
> Because you are precious in my sight,
> and honoured, and I love you...
> Do not fear, for I am with you.
> Isaiah 43:1, 4-5

> I have loved you with an everlasting love therefore
> I have continued my faithfulness to you.
> Jeremiah 31:3

---

[4] *Julian of Norwich: Showings.*

We cannot earn this love – indeed we do not have to earn it. God's love is pure gift, it is already given, freeing us from any demands. God is love (1 John 4:16) God gives Godself in love – in creation, in our everyday lives, and in final fulfilment. God gives us life, sustains us in life, and finally takes us into God's life. In the book of Wisdom, God is called the 'lover of life'. All God wants for us is life:

> In his hand is the life of every living thing
> and the breath of every human being.
> Job 12:10

Even our death opens us to new life, God's life. A friend shared her aunt's prayer when she was close to her death:

> What I don't seem to be able to get my head around
> is that death is part of life.
> Otherwise, you would not have let
> it happen to your Son – or to me.

Death is part of life, integral to life, a way to life. No surprise then that the angels say to the women at the empty tomb 'why do you look for the living amongst the dead?' (Luke 24:5) Jesus died – there were witnesses – but he is alive, alive with God. God is love, God is life.

Here is another story from my ministry. Though I am not a parish priest, I am sometimes called on to help in different pastoral situations. A few years ago, I was asked to help with children's first reconciliation – what the children called confession. Parents brought the children up, one at a time, and left them with me. A boy about seven or eight years old grinned at me and confidently recited: 'these are my sins – I had a fight with my brother'. I said, 'Who won?' which probably confused the poor lad more than helped him. Another fellow about the same age sat in front of me tongue-tied, not a word, for several minutes. I suspect because what he imagined was his big sin was too difficult to say aloud. I tried to assure him not to worry – God knows and God understands.

My only preparation for this ministry was to remind myself to be gentle with the children. Though I understand the importance of children learning the difference between right and wrong, I would want them to know from any early age that they are deeply loved by God, whatever of their 'sins'. Psychologically, it is well established that the messages we pick up when we are young do stay with us, however unconsciously, as we grow older. I know this from personal experience: the message I heard as a child, unspoken in as many words, and I know now unintended, was that I was to be a good boy for my parents. It took many years before I came to see how that had influenced my life. The unconscious motivation in much of my behaviour was to be good and to earn favour. Though my good behaviour was affirmed and praised, that served only to deepen my determination to be good. But I was unaware of my underlying motivation in the way I was living my life. I was not free.

Yet, freedom is God's first gift to us: we are created free. To be human is to be free. In the creation story, God said. 'Let us make humankind in our image, according to our likeness' (Genesis 1:26). To be human is to be loved and to be free. Jesus' words come to mind:

> Look at the birds of the air;
> they neither sow nor reap nor gather into barns,
> and yet your heavenly Father feeds them…
> Consider the lilies of the field and how they grow;
> they neither toil nor spin,
> and yet I tell you,
> even Solomon in all his glory was
> not clothed like one of these.
> Matthew 6:26, 28-29

With that encouragement, all of us desire freedom, we want to be free. And we are. But it seems we are unfree at the same time. As Paul reminded us, 'I do not do the good that I want!' (Romans 7:19). As I ponder how this became the human condition, invariably I am thrown back on those early childhood influences where the emphasis was entirely on our behaviour, overlooking the gift of love already given. Doubtless, this was compounded as we grew up. Maybe not so much today, but in previous days, parents focused on behaviour: be a 'good boy', early schooling, even into adulthood, focused on behaviour: 'these are my sins', church teaching, Sunday sermons, education in morality too frequently focused on behaviour. No one thought to question the behaviour, to look for the motivation underlying the behaviour, whether 'good' or 'bad' behaviour.

There is a clear example, too, for those of us who joined religious communities. The *Rule of St Benedict* was a major influence on the development of religious life. In his rule, Benedict asked the monks to make regular 'manifestation of conscience' to their abbot or to a wise elder. Benedict's intention was clear, but the collateral damage was that the monks – and later other sisters and brothers influenced by Benedict – had to check their external behaviour to ensure they were doing the right thing. This seemed important to earn the abbot's favour, maybe even God's favour. People's inner lives were ignored; even their experience of God's love in their lives was ignored. Many religious people grew up immature, always doing the right thing, but with precious little self-awareness.

This was not St Benedict's intention. It is certainly not God's intention. God created us free and wants us free. And only God can set us free. The scripture passage above is the passage that preceded Jesus' advice that we 'not worry about tomorrow – tomorrow has enough worries of its own!'. The birds of the air do not have to worry about tomorrow because God feeds them. Jesus is saying that we do not have to worry about tomorrow because God cares for us, even more than the birds! While we may well believe that, our behaviour betrays us.

As an aside, I add that freedom does not mean license, as though we can forget all decency and good sense because God makes no demands on us. Rather, when we do truly know this love of God, we have every reason to live well and lead lives that honour God's gift to us. As cited above, Julian of Norwich believed that this was the greatest honour we can give God. Our response from the heart comes quite spontaneously. We say thankyou.

My emphasis on the *gift* of life is intentional. When writing of gratefulness – 'the root of joy is gratefulness' – David Steindl-Rast coined a phrase 'the illusion of entitlement', reminding us how easily we can take for granted what really is gift. As though we are entitled to what comes our way.[5] This seems important to me not only when reflecting on God's gifts, but on the many gifts we receive daily from other people. Maybe that is how God's gifts come – through other people's kindness. The smile or the little wave as I pass a person I have never met is too easily taken for granted.

When we know the depth of God's gift of love for us on a personal level, then Jesus' encouragement to love one another seems almost natural. Not only because we know that others are equally loved by God, but also because we want to pass on the gift. 'Love one another as I have loved you.' Years ago, a friend said to me that 'love is never wasted'. The years have convinced me of the truth of that time and time again. Love is never wasted; it always bears good fruit. Experiencing God's love, I become more loving myself. My attitude to others, my relationships with others become more accepting, more tolerant, more loving. Such is the gift.

---

5 David Steindl-Rast, *Gratefulness: the Heart of Prayer* (Mahwah, N.J.: Paulist Press, 1984).

Some go so far as to say that everything is gift. Yes and No. For example, as discussed in what follows, I do not believe that cancer is God's gift. I do not believe that earthquakes and tsunamis are gifts from God. Rather, much in our everyday experience is the result of a human mistake somewhere along the line. God is not to be blamed for what we have caused by our ignorance and stupidity. In fact, God has given us the wherewithal, the intelligence and the expertise to prevent such calamities in our lives, to recover from them, and even to benefit from them. They can bring out the best in people: courage, compassion, care for one another. All of which are surely gifts from God.

We remain gifted. Gratitude is the basic Christian attitude: God is the giver, we are the receivers – we say thankyou. Our lives become a thankyou to God. We live in gratitude.

Chapter Two

Living in Gratitude

To live in gratitude for God's gift in our lives, as noted, my first suggestion is to downplay negativity, the things we have done wrong, and the emphasis on doing the right thing. Then, equally importantly, we make God's love and the daily reminders of God's care our first focus, deepening our appreciation of the gift.

A beautiful example of focusing on God's gifts is the popular Louis Armstrong song *A Wonderful World*. First recorded in 1967, the lyrics are no less relevant today. Despite racial discrimination, anxiety around climate change, and a scary pandemic, we live in a wonderful world. We still find hope in our world.

Louis Armstrong found the first evidence of our wonderful world in creation:

> *I see trees of green, red roses too*
> *I see them bloom for me and you*
> *And I think to myself what a wonderful world*
>
> *I see skies of blue and clouds of white*
> *The bright blessed day and the dark sacred night*
> *And I think to myself what a wonderful world*

There is much more he could have added – from the beauty of birds and trees and seas, to the evolution of species and the expanding solar system, all the miracles of creation, the gifts of God's love.[6]

Most people do seem more aware of creation in recent times, doubtless helped by the good publicity being given to how easily and how frequently we damage God's creation – as in the exploitation of the earth's resources, the denudation of forests, and the pollution of the earth and the atmosphere.

In his encyclical *Laudato Si'*, Pope Francis points out that much of the destruction has come about because of the presumption that human beings dominate creation, as though creation exists for the sake of humanity. The ecological conversion that the Pope calls for, rather, believes in mutual responsibility with creation. We depend on creation, as it depends on us; we care for creation, as it cares for us. Our caring for creation, then, is not from a position of dominance, but of oneness.

For many years, I lived on a large rural property near the sea. One of the gifts of the time was that I became more aware of the changing seasons, the recurring patterns and indicators of approaching weather, the movement of the tides, and the beauty of my surrounds. I contemplated the sea daily, I was entertained by the playful bird and animal

---

6 See, for example, Denis Edwards, *Jesus and the Natural World* (Mulgrave, Vic: Garratt Publishing, 201

life outside the window of my quiet space, and I eagerly anticipated the cycle of blossoms and colours in my garden.

I was but one member of this earthly community. I used to say that I lived with a beautiful fox who once ventured onto my front lawn, a black wallaby in the bush, an echidna who often visited the back yard, a few koalas, many possums and rabbits, my chickens and my Kelpie companion, Scobie. We were well aware of one another and respected one another's right to be there: we lived in harmony. In the mutuality and inter-relatedness of such a community – sometimes only fleetingly – I sensed our shared life, our communion. Dare I call this shared life God's life?

Pope Francis does: all creation shares God's life. All creation is sacred, made so from the very beginning in God's very act of creation, by Jesus shedding his blood poured into our earth, and by the Spirit of God who finally transforms and reconciles all. We praise God's life in creation as we sing *What a wonderful world* we live in.

The same sentiment is found in numerous religious songs. The beautiful hymn *How Great Thou Art* (1885) sings *awesome wonder* before God's creation. James McAuley's *Creation sings a new song unto the Lord* (1999) repeats a refrain praising God for creation: *creation praises and reflects the wisdom of God.*

But Armstrong did not stop with creation. God created people, too:

The colours of the rainbow, so pretty in the sky
And also on the faces of people going by
I see friends shaking hands saying how do you do
But they're really saying I love you

I hear babies cry and I watch them grow
They'll learn much more than I'll ever know
And I think to myself what a wonderful world
Yes, I think to myself what a wonderful world

As the people of God, we are all equal and equally loved by God. This is the basis of our love for one another. Just as all creation is one, all people are one, whatever of differing backgrounds, skin colours, beliefs and ways of life. Whatever of differences, we have much in common. We share God's love. The song acknowledges this: people shaking hands are really expressing love for one another. Granted that we greet others individually and differently, I am a strong believer in handshakes. We do not say the words 'I love you' to everyone we meet, but our handshake, our hug when appropriate, gives the same message.

When we have the experience of being known and loved personally by someone, our awareness of God's love for us moves to an even deeper level. For many people, this intimate experience of knowing love is beyond words, beyond thankyous. I think of the unique loving relationship that St Thomas More enjoyed with his daughter Margaret, often called Meg. In his desire to comfort his daughter in her distress as More approached his execution on Tower Hill in London (1535), More said to her 'you alone have long known the secrets of my heart'.

More is speaking of their unique, intimate relationship, their bonding of hearts. Far from mere intellectual knowing, this is wholistic knowing, to know in one's whole person. Margaret alone knew her father's deep inner life, his 'secrets', his profound relationship with God. She thanked him once for a letter which she said represented to her 'the clear shining brightness of your soul'. She alone knew and understood how More was able to oppose the King, despite enormous pressure to do otherwise and despite his crippling fears for himself and for his family.

The primacy of his relationship with God – 'I am the King's good servant, but God's first' – was non-negotiable for More. Clearly, Thomas More knew in his heart God's personal love for him. In some sense, we could all say the same` – we are all loved, maybe no big secret, but not all of us are able to say to one other person 'you alone know the secrets of my heart.' For Thomas More and for Meg – and for others who share their experience – it is surely a wonderful world.

What a wonderful world is a song of gratitude. As we deepen our awareness of God's gifts in our lives, in creation and in other people, we say thankyou.

Gratitude is uppermost in another song: renowned singer/ songwriter, inductee in the ARIA Hall of Fame, Olivia Newton-John, released her album called *Grace and Gratitude* in 2006. The title song *Grace and Gratitude* celebrates:

*I stand here in grace and gratitude:
all I have and all I feel is all because of you.*

The words *I thank you* are repeated several times, ending with *Thankyou for life, Thankyou for everything*. Remembering that Newton-John had recurring bouts of cancer in her life, I see this as honest, gutsy prayer.

Indeed, this is the key to honest prayer: prayer that looks and listens to God and God's presence and God's gifts in our life. When we do this, such prayer overflows into the way we live our lives: we become more loving people, more caring of others. Olivia Newton-John's own experience attests this: she gave considerable time and energy (and the proceeds of her song) to works of charity. Our lives become our thankyou.

I have suggested already that our prayer will help us to grow in inner freedom. I say this because I suspect that our understanding of prayer and our approach to prayer may also have suffered from early education. In the vocal prayers many of us were taught as children, we learned to concentrate and to say the right words – surely then, God will hear us! This approach seemed to depend on our having the right words and the right way to pray – again, the emphasis was decidedly on our effort. Not only in childhood. Many of us suffered from the same emphasis when, later, we were introduced to meditative prayer. Meditation, especially meditation of the Sacred Scriptures, involves clear thinking on our part, working out what the passage is saying and asking of us. But again, the emphasis is on our work, not God's work in us. I know that for many of us, this way of praying failed to satisfy after some time. When that happens, the best advice is to slow down, not work so hard, sit still and wait and listen. This seems to be how we are led from meditative prayer to what traditionally is called contemplative prayer (though I notice that it is still called meditation in some circles).

Francis de Sales' book *Treatise on the Love of God*, referred to above, describes this transition from meditative prayer to contemplative prayer. When our focus is on God's love in our lives, a more contemplative prayer, listening, waiting, receiving, seems to happen even without our planning.

An example of contemplative prayer in this way is our daily review of each day. Rather than trying to remember every hour of the day, better to ask God to remind us where God has been in my life today. Then we wait on God's word, not our own assessment of the day. The Bible encourages us to do this. There is a lovely story in the Book of Exodus where Moses says to God: 'show me your face' to which God replied:

> I will be gracious to whom I will be gracious,
> and will show mercy on whom I will show mercy.
> But you cannot see my face, for
> no one shall see me and live.
> See, there is a place by me where
> you shall stand on the rock;
> and while my glory passes by, I
> will put you in a cleft of the rock,
> and I will cover you with my hand until I have passed by.

> Then I will take away my hand,
> and you shall see my back...
> Exodus 33:19-23

Almost playfully, God tells Moses that he cannot see God face to face, but he can see God's back. In another translation, 'you will see where I have been'.

It makes good sense to look back on each day to see 'where I have been'. I have found it a very worthwhile habit to have cultivated. At the end of each day, I quietly ask God to remind me where God has been for me during the day, where was God loving me today, maybe that I didn't notice at the time.

Such contemplative prayer will invite gratitude and praise of God. As well, it will make us more sensitive to how God gifts us – and it will gradually free us, because it leaves us open to God's working in us. When we persevere with this way of prayer, we don't necessarily notice any change happening in us, but in time we will notice that we have indeed changed. We become freer people and our way of life is the better for it.

I have written extensively about this in two other books *The Eyes of God* and *The Joy of Ageing*.[7] It is the prayer called *The Awareness Examen*. It is the best help I know for us to learn God's ways, the ways that God is present and gifting us in our lives. Gratitude flows spontaneously. In my

---

[7] Brian Gallagher msc, *The Eyes of God* (2019) and *The Joy of Ageing* (2020), both published by Coventry Press, Bayswater, Vic.

experience, I say thankyou so often that it becomes a way of life. Hence my phrase 'living in gratitude'.

Chapter Three

But...

But, I hear you saying, the world we live in is not 100% wonderful. So many things seem wrong in our world that sometimes we wonder whether God has abandoned us. People are dying of hunger, countries are being swallowed up by rising sea levels, refugees are being left in limbo for years, and our church is severely bruised as she slowly comes to terms with revelations of scandal, abuse and cover-up, already impacting on reduced numbers of attendees and loss of standing in the community. How can we be grateful for these things?

Having expressed our gratitude for all the wonderful things in our world, we must also face these painful, less-than-happy experiences. As I am confronted by the reality of our world with its many questions and few answers, I have discovered surprisingly that there may yet be blessing. Something new may be emerging in our world and in our church. A new life that we will surely be grateful for.

I base this on the writing of a Carmelite Sister called Constance Fitzgerald, who was the first to recognise that the personal experience that John of the Cross called a 'dark night' happens also on a communal level, in society and in church. She named genocide and marginalisation of women world-wide as examples. Fitzgerald called the experience *impasse*, when there appears to be no way out, no rational escape, and no turning back from the situation we find ourselves in. Indeed, when the temptation for some is to give up, to surrender to despair and hopelessness. This describes well where we find ourselves today. As we face those painful experiences I have listed, it does indeed seem like a dark night, the term 'dark' referring to our helplessness and our uncertainty about what lies ahead. As in a real dark night, we cannot see our way clearly. This is precisely John of the Cross' meaning.

But, Fitzgerald says:

> what if, by chance, our time in evolution is a 'dark night' time – a time of crisis and transition that must be understood if it is to be part of learning a new vision and harmony for the human species and the planet?[8]

John of the Cross would say that, paradoxically, a situation of no apparent potential, in fact, is loaded with potential, that God brings new life to us when we seem to be at a dead end.[9] He teaches that in the very experience of darkness and joylessness, in the suffering and withdrawal of the satisfaction and pleasure we were accustomed to, a

---

8 Constance Fitzgerald, 'Impasse and Dark Night' in *Living with Apocalypse*, ed. Tilden H. Edwards (San Francisco, CA: Harper & Row, 1984) 94.

9 John of the Cross, 'Dark Night' in *The Collected Works of St. John of the Cross*, ed. Kieran Kavanaugh & Otilio Rodriguez (Washington, DC: Institute of Carmelite Studies, 1973)

transformation is taking place. John says that dark night is new life, an experience of grace, of consolation (admittedly that doesn't feel very consoling). John says it is a time when we are being purified, when egoism dies and unselfish love for another is set free, when we are challenged to move from loving others because of the joy it gives us, to loving others for their sake, regardless of the cost to ourselves. Strange as it sounds, even in this dark time we are again being gifted by God. It is a time for trusting God, a time of deepening relationship with God.

All of which can happen on a communal level. Fitzgerald's examples were the holocaust suffered by Jewish people, genocide in Bosnia and elsewhere, and women's experience of social and ecclesial marginalisation. My current examples are climate change, unjust detention of refugees, and sexual abuse in the church – in all of which the argument proposed by John of the Cross and Constance Fitzgerald applies in the same way. This is a time of 'darkness and joylessness' in our church and our world when many ask 'where is God in these times?'

Elie Wiesel tells the story of a cruel hanging of a young child in a Jewish concentration camp, that all camp residents were obliged to witness. As they watched the child hanging, dying on the gallows, a loud voice from the crowd called out 'where is God now?' Wiesel recounts that his response came from deep within himself: 'God is hanging on those gallows'. Wiesel is saying that in some sense God suffers with us, God grieves, God dislikes the loss of human life as much as we do. God promises new life.

Before we recognise any new life that might be emerging, it seems important that we take on board our experience of impasse, that we acknowledge that we are limited and powerless to change what is happening for us communally, in society and in church, and that we are willing to surrender to the mystery, the unknown future. We will feel the pain of the present experience before we know any of God's gift. The new will emerge from the pain, the helplessness and the uncertainty.

As we trust God's ever-present love in our lives, doubtless with mixed emotion, John of the Cross says that new life in our dying will surely emerge. Without denying the reality of those harsh times, the things that we find impossible to be grateful for, I believe that there are signs of new life emerging already. I sense a new, more wholesome appreciation of creation and our oneness with creation emerging. I think there is a new awareness of our brotherhood and our sisterhood, our care for one another emerging. Maybe, hopefully, even a new, truer, more humble church is emerging.

I acknowledge that Fitzgerald's examples – and mine – are somewhat dramatic: genocide, world famine, rampant sexual abuse in the church. Closer to home, I think of more personal examples that I suspect are others' experience, as well.

For example, who does not have unfulfilled dreams in their life, plans worked hard to achieve, but that never eventuated? I read recently that 'life is what keeps happening to you while you are busy making other plans' (reputed to John Lennon). I can identify with that.

A very moving example is Fantine's song *I dreamed a dream* in the musical *Les Misêrables*. Fantine is the tragic figure, maybe the most 'miserable' of *Les Misêrables* in Victor Hugo's 1862 novel. Fantine's story includes being abandoned as a child, falling pregnant as a teenager to a student who promptly leaves her, finding herself unable to care for her daughter Cosette and leaving her with a couple she barely knew, losing her job and ending up as a prostitute, dying of tuberculosis at a young age without seeing Cosette again.

Anne Hathaway's singing in the movie of the story seems to me to capture Fantine's anguish, pain and hopelessness as if it were her own. I dreamed a dream – 'and then it all went wrong':

> *I dreamed a dream in time gone by*
> *When hope was high and life worth living*
> *I dreamed that love would never die*
> *I dreamed that God would be forgiving ...*

And then it all went wrong:

> *But the tigers came at night*
> *With their voices soft as thunder*
> *As they tear your hope apart*
> *As they turn your dream to shame ...*

Fantine's painful song ends with:

> *I had a dream that life would be*
> *So different from the hell I'm living*
> *So different now from what it seemed*

Now life has killed the dream
I dreamed

In the story, that is how Fantine died. She was saved from the streets and was well cared for in her dying days, but she died with her unfulfilled dream, her unfulfilled life, worse for her, a life like living in hell.

I feel compassion for Fantine, symbolic of the many others who have suffered similarly, but whose story has never been told. As we hear and take people's stories on board, I believe that we grow in love and compassion. Our world is the better.

As I live with my own unfulfilled dreams and my prayer for others in similar, even more painful places, I remind myself that, in God's way, 'all things work together for good' (Romans 8:28). I may not see the good, but I am invited to trust God's work. This doesn't take away the disappointment, but maybe it can remind us that God may have more in store for us. Often I have had to let go of a dream or a hope, but invariably I have found that I am more than happy with what did happen. I could be thankful for an outcome that, in fact, was far removed from my own vision. The letting go is the dying, the outcome is the new life.

In different imagery, Andrew Lloyd Webber talks of the same experience of dark night in the song *The Music of the Night* from *The Phantom of the Opera*. This song, too, has become a favourite of mine, inviting me/us to a deeper level of living.

In the first verse, we hear that in night time, *silently our senses abandon their defences*. For most of us, most of the time, our senses and the emotions they trigger tell us what we judge to be reality – we see and we touch, we taste and we smell – and we consider that what our senses tell us, in fact, is reality. The wisdom of the song is rather that, when the senses *abandon their defences*, then our awareness sharpens and opens us to new possibilities. Our senses do have 'defences', their inbuilt tendency to insist that they – our seeing, touching, tasting and smelling – are enough to show us truth and life. It seems that, only when we can see beyond our senses, only then does deeper truth and truer life become possible. That happens in *night time*, the time when it is too dark to see and touch, taste and smell.

The darkness of night time *heightens* and *sharpens* our senses: though it is too 'dark' to see or taste, we still say that we 'sense' something happening or we sense someone's presence (even when we cannot see or touch, taste or smell). In other words, we begin to 'sense' in a whole different way, a deeper, truer way. The following verses tell us something of what this difference is – what is this deeper way of 'sensing'?

'Night' has its own music: the music of the night. The song tells us that this music is *tremulous and tender*, yet with its own *splendour*. If we are to discover that splendour, *tremulous and tender* suggests that we need to listen carefully, gently, respectfully. We could easily miss the music. Indeed, I suspect we will miss it if we listen with our physical ear only. The music being offered to us is a very different kind of music, a music somehow beyond (not heard by) our usual hearing (or seeing, touching, tasting).

In the darkness of the night, our everyday senses will hear only silence: the music we are accustomed to hearing will seem to be absent. Indeed, *purge your thoughts of the life you knew before*. If we are to hear the music of the night, the song suggests that we need to let go of our past experience – what we have always thought to be music, and enjoyed. Let go of the past, because we are being invited to listen now on the level of 'spirit'. *Let your spirit soar* – and you are in for a big surprise, 'a strange new world' of experience, a life *as you've never lived before*.

In this new life, living in the Spirit, all we have are our 'spiritual senses': we listen 'with the ear of the heart', in St Benedict's phrase; we see 'with the eyes of God', as I have written elsewhere describing the prophet. Best of all, we have a 'nose for the things of God'. It is indeed a strange new world.

How do we understand this world of the spirit? What would it mean 'to live in the Spirit'? The song says this is *where you long to be*. I know that I long for what is good and true, for wholeness and for love, which I imagine is fairly universal human longing. But I know, too, that what I long for is not within my reach. My effort to find these values – symbolised by my use of my senses – eventually has to surrender to the *darkness you know you cannot fight*. Then I have to wait, believing that what I long for will eventually be given to me. Indeed, we remember that the gift has already been given. It has been given in night time, when I am barely aware it is happening. And so, *The Music of the Night* encourages us to *let the music caress you, hear it, feel it, secretly possess you* – let the music (of the night) do its work in me.

Again I turn to John of the Cross who speaks of the same experience in his poem *After an Ecstasy*:

> *I went into an unknown land*
> *unknowing, stayed there knowing naught,*
> *beyond the power of human thought.*
>
> *I know not where I entered in*
> *But when I found that I was there,*
> *not knowing how, not knowing where,*
> *strange things I heard, so deep within,*
> *far greater than I could declare.*
> *So there I stayed still knowing naught,*
> *far, far beyond all human thought.*[10]

This is the *strange new world* of the song. I suspect that few of us call it 'ecstasy', but it is to live 'in the spirit', to live as we've 'never lived before', to live truly believing that there is light in darkness, life in death, God's gift to us. Once again, an invitation to gratitude.

---

10 John of the Cross, *Centered on Love: the Poems of St John of the Cross*, translated by Marjorie Flower (Varroville, NSW: the Carmelite Nuns, 1983, reprinted 2002, 27).

Chapter Four

Life in Death

I experience a further challenge to our wonderful world when confronted by war: war amongst people, the death and destruction God's people inflict on one another.

Some years ago, I celebrated my Golden Jubilee as a Missionary of the Sacred Heart with a musical concert. A number of friends performed items by request. One was Eric Bogle's *The Band played Waltzing Matilda*. Bogle, Scottish by birth, Australian by adoption, wrote this piece in 1971 at the height of the Vietnam war, though he situated his story in the First World War. He wanted to speak of the futility of war – the obvious reason that I identify with the lyrics so easily.

I find the music quite haunting as the lyrics tell the tragic story of the Australian army's defeat at Gallipoli in 1917.

The futility of war is maybe best captured in these verses:

> *How well I remember that terrible day*
> *How our blood stained the sand and the water*
> *And how on that hell that they called Suvia Bay*
> *We were butchered like lambs at the slaughter...*
> *But the band played Waltzing Matilda*

> *So they gathered the crippled, the wounded, the maimed*
> *And they shipped us home to Australia...*
> *And as our ship pulled into Circular Quay*
> *I looked at the place where my legs used to be*
> *And thanked Christ there was nobody waiting for me*
> *to grieve, to mourn and to pity*
> *But the band played Waltzing Matilda*

Near the end of the song, Bogle sings of the annual Anzac Day parades:

> *I sit on me porch*
> *And I watch the parades pass me by...*
> *And young people ask 'what are they marching for?'*
> *And I ask myself the same question*
> *But the band played Waltzing Matilda*

Ah, the futility of war.

There may well be 'a time for peace and a time for war' (Eccles. 3:8) – I cannot see it. There may well be possibility of 'a just war' – I would give anything to find another way of solving disagreements. The reality of war frightens me, I cannot fathom the conditions under which those soldiers fought, their fears, their suffering, the sheer agony of fighting and killing other men and women, the pointless loss of life. I know I could not do it. I could not kill another person. *The Band played Waltzing Matilda* says all of this. but more powerfully coming from the mouth of someone who was there, fighting in the trenches, watching mates die, even while seriously wounded himself. Does he say we live in a wonderful world?

While decrying the futility of war, the song becomes a tribute to the Anzacs at the same time. Bogle has the accompaniment playing *Waltzing Matilda*, that quintessential Australian bush ballad, throughout the saga – initially, as the army confidently embarks, amid the cheers of families and friends on the quay, but then again on their sad return, grieving their dead and nursing their sick. The band plays *Waltzing Matilda* during the soldiers' courageous landing at Gallipoli, despite the barrage of Turkish bullets and shells, but then again on their equally courageous retreat, diminished and defeated.

Waltzing Matilda, if nothing else, reminds all that we are Australian. Stand tall, be proud, we are Australian. There is rich irony here: while I find war horrid, I cannot help but admire the courage and the generosity of the women and men who fight for their country. I attend Anzac Day service every year and I rejoice in the pride of the marching diggers, the survivors, and their happy reunions. I share the sad grieving of the families who have lost loved ones and I hear their bitter-sweet memories. I shed a tear as I hear the ode and the Last Post:

> They shall not grow old, as we who are left grow old.
> Age shall not weary them, nor the years condemn.
> At the going down of the sun, and in the morning,
> we will remember them.
> Lest we forget.[11]

---

11 Laurence Binyon, *For the Fallen* poem, published in *The Times* newspaper 21 September 1914.

What are they marching for? is a reasonable question. I think their answer would be something like: 'we are remembering our mates who did not survive but gave their lives, the many buried in foreign lands (some thousands in Australian war cemeteries in several countries, but sadly many in unknown, unmarked graves we cannot even visit.) This is our tribute to them. Lest we forget'.

Waltzing Matilda can be a mournful song and a jubilant song at the same time.

The same irony calls Anzac Day our national day. A day of defeat has become a day of celebration in Australia. This mystifies some people, but I see it as fitting: there is a humility in defeat or failure. We are invited to admit our mistakes and to acknowledge our weaknesses. Our best efforts do not necessarily carry the day – we discover quickly that we need a higher power. We learn and we become stronger people in defeat. We are not defeated by defeat. I recall the words of the Muslim Imam after the massacre of Muslim people in their synagogue in Auckland some years ago: we are broken-hearted, but we are not broken. For good reason, *The Band played Waltzing Matilda*. Even in war, even in defeat, we find there can still be gratitude. Once again, we discover there is life in death. Maybe we are better people for having had the experience of war also.

A favourite image of Jesus comes back to me. Pilate presents Jesus to the crowds, crowned, mocked, alone, to all appearances defeated: *Ecce Homo* – 'Here is the man' (John 19:5). Before Pilate and before the crowds, Jesus remains silent, more self-assured, more certain of his place than anyone else in the scene. Paradoxically, I see Jesus' life fulfilled in that moment of apparent emptiness and aloneness.

Personally, I can acknowledge many blessings in my life. Yes, even while I count my blessings – which I do often – I also experience a kind of hollowness in my life, an aloneness that seems to be at the very core of who I am. And is ever-present. There seems to be a deep place inside me that no other person ever touches – and that, despite all those blessings, all the wonderful friends, all the apparently fruitful ministry.

Whenever events or experiences put me in touch with my aloneness, I have learned that I need to choose it. I used to fight it, even imagine that I was badly done by. Now I face it head-on – I choose to accept it. I now see this inner core of who I am as a very precious place, a place to treasure and care for – dare I say – a place of God. Yes, I feel alone, but I'm discovering that that is not the whole story. Something else is emerging.

I know the same experience in my prayer. As I sit before God, more often than not I find myself empty of thoughts and emotions. I seem barely present, aware of my breathing but little else. I identify with Cistercian monk, Thomas Merton's description of the apparent emptiness he experiences in prayer – apparently, many people know the same. Merton cautions that 'the emptiness is only apparent':

> The absence of activity... is only apparent. Below the surface, the mind and will are drawn into the orbit of an activity that is deep and intense and supernatural, and which overflows into our whole being and brings forth incalculable fruits.[12]

The fruits that Merton promises, in fact, are God's gifts of growth in inner freedom and truth, emerging out of the apparent emptiness or darkness. John of the Cross' teaching on the experience of 'dark night', cited above, would suggest the same:

> (The dark night) is the secret way in which God not only liberates us from our attachments and idolatries, but also brings us to the realisation of our true nature. The night is the means by which we find our heart's desire, our freedom for love.[13]

In God's way, new life is the constant promise: there is always life in the dying. I daresay this is why many have said that 'silence is the language of God'. God may well seem silent – and often does – but God's silence is God's way of communicating! We are invited to deeper faith, trusting that something is happening in us deep-down.

As if to encourage me, God has given me glimpses of that promised strength and acceptance: times when I have known beyond doubt that I am alone, but not alone. At

---

12 Thomas Merton, *Seeds of Contemplation* (Wheathampstead, Hertfordshire: Anthony Clarke Books, 1961), 188.
13 Gerald May, *The Dark Night of the Soul*, (San Francisco, CA: Harper SanFrancisco, 2004), 67.

those times, I identify with the words of John of the Cross in his poem, *The Spiritual Canticle*:

> *You looked with love upon me*
> *and deep within, your eyes imprinted grace.*
> *This mercy set me free,*
> *held in your love's embrace,*
> *to life my eyes adoring to your face.*[14]

The joyful emotion of such times doesn't last. But occasional glimpses are enough: I may long for a repeat or a deeper experience, but my knowing does not depend on that. Most of the time, the invitation is to keep believing that God's gift to me is ever present, even when all I am aware of is my aloneness and the emptiness of my prayer. Seen with different eyes, maybe I can say that the aloneness is somehow transformed – not taken away, but it seems imbued with new hope. John of the Cross says 'with love'.

Maybe Aunty's prayer is relevant here, too: 'what I don't seem to be able to get my head around is that death is part of life'. Just as death is an opening to new life, might not the hardships many of our sisters and brothers are experiencing and our own more personal experiences of letting go our dreams also be openings to something new. God desires only life for God's people. God will surely gift us again with an even deeper grace of gratitude.

---

14 John of the Cross, *Centered on Love*, 20.

Chapter Five

Resurrection

The same dynamic of life emerging from death, inviting trust and gratitude, was preached by Archbishop Oscar Romero of San Salvador, now St Oscar, before he was murdered during Mass in 1980. Romero's parting words were:

> If God accepts the sacrifice of my life, may my death be for the freedom of my people. A bishop will die, but the Church of God, which is the people, will never perish. I do not believe in death without resurrection. If they kill me, I will rise again in the people of El Salvador.[15]

Romero's conviction that he will rise again in the people of El Salvador captures the basic Christian paradox: death and new life. It is the way that Jesus taught and lived, and how he died. Dying and rising belong together. Death is part of life.

In all post-Resurrection stories, Jesus' message to his disciples was one of encouragement: 'Why are you frightened and why do doubts arise in your hearts?' (Luke 24:38). 'Peace be to you. As the Father has sent me, so I send

---

15 This was cited in my book *The Joy of Ageing* (Bayswater Vic: Coventry Press, 2021).

you' (John 20:21). Jesus is encouraging us to take heart, to live confidently – because of his death and resurrection.

There is a beautiful French icon that has become popular in my religious community. The icon depicts Jesus appearing to Mary and the frightened disciples in the locked room. As Jesus shows them his pierced hands and his heart, the caption says 'être sur terre le coeur de Dieu', translated as 'to be on earth the heart of God'. This is Jesus' message – knowing that he is now risen from the dead makes it possible for the disciples, for us, 'to be on earth the heart of God'. We are invited to live God's heart, God's love and compassion. All that we are and all that we do will witness God's love. Indeed, God loves in us. Our very loving another is God loving, expressed in our relationships, the way we relate to other people.

I have recalled examples of my ministry in earlier chapters. When I celebrated my Golden Jubilee of priesthood, I described my ministry for fifty years as predominately a ministry of presence to people, listening, supporting, encouraging, forgiving and asking forgiveness, guiding, praying. Whether in pastoral situations, in the years of seminary formation and guidance of young students, or in the subsequent years of spiritual direction and retreat work, or the teaching and supervision of other spiritual directors, I have wanted to be present to others in personal ways. This led to my emphasis on the place of and value of relationships in my life. Relationships, I acknowledge, that find their value in my underlying relationship with God. The 16th century Carmelite mystic, John of the Cross, cited above, wrote another poem called *The Living Flame of Love*. This is the last verse:

> *Ah! Gentle and so loving*
> *You wake within me, proving*
> *that you are there, in secret and alone.*
> *Your fragrant breathing stills me*
> *Your grace, your glory fills me*
> *So tenderly, your love becomes my own.*[16]

'Your love becomes my own' captures the subtitle of this book: that is precisely our way of life.

Jesus' disciples heard the message. In their early Church preaching, invariably their emphasis was that the Jesus whom you crucified, God has raised up – '*and we are the witnesses to this*' (for example Acts 2:32 – the emphasis is mine). They could not have meant 'witnesses' in the legal sense of being able to swear on the Bible that they saw it happen. But maybe in this sense that their very standing there preaching confidently witnesses God's gift of resurrection to Jesus.

Not surprisingly, the death to life paradox appears also in music. The best example for me is Gustav Mahler's *Resurrection Symphony*. Mahler's second symphony took him six years to compose (1888-1894). The composer acknowledged that the delay in finishing was caused by his search for a fitting final movement – Mahler wanted a choral finale to capture resurrection and life in death. He found it finally in a poem called *The Resurrection* by fellow German Friedrich Klopstock.

---

16 John of the Cross, *Centered on Love*, 23.

The symphony is quite lengthy, in five movements. The first movement is made up of funeral rites, death with all its questions. The music is sombre, grave, at times strident. One senses Mahler's own question: is there any life after death? The music suggests maybe not. I find it quite disturbing. After an extended pause, the orchestra then begins the second much slower movement, suggesting that the deceased's life has not been all doom and gloom – there are quieter happy memories. But this mood doesn't last – quickly the third movement arrives, seeming to question it all – what does life mean? This movement climaxes in what Mahler himself called 'a cry of despair'. Listening, it is almost as if there is nowhere else to go at this point – it *is* despairing. This early section of the symphony parallels our experience of the hard times when we seem to have no place to go to relieve the sadness and struggle in our world, as discussed above.

The despairing mood is relieved only by the introduction of the chorus in the fourth movement. The music becomes more solemn, thoughtful, as a soloist sings a longing theme, longing for relief from the world's troubles and struggles. Maher seems to be saying 'is there yet some hope?' It was at this point, apparently, that he delayed further writing as he searched – or waited for inspiration – for a fifth movement. When the inspiration came via Klopstock's poem, Mahler's choral movement is in striking contrast to the earlier movements.

This fifth movement begins with repetition of many earlier themes, even the earlier 'cry of despair' – this is the background, the context in which we are invited to wait for resurrection. At last, an eerie off-stage trumpet intones the resurrection call, suggesting something new is emerging. Mahler called this 'the great summons'. I can hear it as I write. The program notes supplied by the Melbourne Symphony Orchestra describe what happens next: 'The most magical moment of all arrives'. A solo soprano soars above the chorus with the resurrection promise:

> *Rise again, thou shall rise again*
> *My dust, after brief rest*
> *Immortal life, Immortal life*
> *He who calleth thee will grant thee*

Then the 'magical moment' does arrive for me:

> *O believe, my heart, O believe*
> *All is not lost with thee*
> *Thine is what thou hast yearned for*
> *Thine what thou hast loved*
> *What thou hast fought for*

In another translation, *Thine is what thou hast yearned for* is translated as: *what you have longed for is yours*, words that have never left me. Through the remainder of this final movement, as I listen, invariably overcome with awe and tearful gratitude, *what you have longed for is yours* sits gently on my heart. The chorus sings:

> *O believe,*
> *Thou wert not born in vain*
> *Hast not lived in vain Suffered in vain!*
> *Prepare thyself to live!*

Mahler's climax comes with urgency and emphasis, sung by all voices:

> *I shall die, to live! I shall die, to live!*

Again, we affirm 'death is part of life'. The soprano has the last word:

> *Rise again, yes rise again*
> *With thee, my heart, in the twinkling of an eye*
> *What thou hast fought for*
> *Shall lead thee to God!*

The final orchestral flourish, all stops out, including organ and bells, celebrates our resurrected life. We celebrate resurrection, not as something to look forward to, but as a gift already given – resurrection has already happened: *What you have longed for is yours*.

The challenge is to believe that our risen life has already been given to us: *What you have longed for is yours*. There is no greater gift. We say thankyou. With such encouragement, our trusting God surely is beyond question.

Chapter Six

Trust in God

On what do we base our trust in another person? We trust the mechanic who services our car, we trust the restaurant chef who prepares our meal. We are invited to trust God through our lives: 'I know the one in whom I have put my trust' (2 Timothy 1:12).

I suggest that we trust the mechanic because of his experience and his good name amongst the many who give him their business. We trust the chef because of his reputation and standing in the industry. We know these people are trustworthy. We trust God for similar reasons: we know that God is trustworthy for God has always cared for us:

> The Lord your God carried you, just as one carries a child, all the way that you travelled until you reached this place.
>
> Deuteronomy 1:31

Any possibility of trust in God is based on our conviction that God has cared for us until now.

Such trust is captured beautifully in Newman's prayer *Lead Kindly Light*. John Henry Newman, Anglican priest, later Catholic priest and cardinal, now Saint, composed the words of the poem *Lead Kindly Light* in 1833. He had been stranded in Italy for some weeks with sickness. Longing to return to England, Newman finally found passage on a small boat. He wrote the poem on that voyage, presumably not a particularly easy voyage, though some commentators suggest that the poem may also refer to his struggle with his faith commitment around that same time. His conversion from Anglicanism to Catholicism came some years later.

In this prayer, Newman initially outlines the difficult situation that he finds himself in and acknowledges that he has not always trusted God's care. Finally he recognises that, in fact, God has always cared for him – there is no reason to think that that will change. I see the key to the prayer in the line *So long thy power hath blessed me* in the last verse.

Keeping our memory of God's care for us alive and uppermost saves us from the risk of taking God's gifts for granted. Our memories of the many ways that we have been blessed are held in our heart, as Mary MacKillop reminded us.

Here is Newman's prayer, initially depicting his desire to trust:

> *Lead kindly light amid the encircling gloom*
> *Lead thou me on*
> *The night is dark and I am far from home*
> *Lead thou me on*
> *Keep thou my feet, I do not ask to see*
> *The distant scene, one step enough for me*

Clearly at the time, Newman knew only gloom, darkness, distant outcome. He believed his only hope was to trust in a higher power. *Light* contrasts with the darkness he was experiencing (the dark night), and *Kindly Light* expresses his hope that this power – God – would treat him favourably and lead him through the darkness. Putting our trust in a greater power is reminiscent of the prayer of Alcoholics Anonymous, which says quite explicitly that only a power greater than ourselves can save us.

Newman's poem is thought to be based on Exodus 13:21-22 which describes how God led the chosen people in a pillar of cloud by day and a pillar of fire by night. Newman prays to be led in the same way. I wonder how frequently he prayed this prayer, even after his return to England and his conversion to Catholicism.

On record is that the prayer has been sung in some very drastic situations of need and trust in God – for example, in the Ravensbruck concentration camp, on the sinking *Titanic*, and by miners in Durham trapped underground, hoping for rescue.

That we do not always enjoy our dependence on God – indeed that we sometimes fight against it – is captured in Newman's second verse:

> *I was not ever thus nor prayed that thou*
> *shouldst lead me on*
> *I loved to choose, to see my path, but now*
> *Lead thou me on*
> *I loved the garish day, and spite of fears*
> *Pride ruled my will, remember not past years*

Newman is acknowledging that he was not always trusting. His past desire to be the one *to choose, to see my path* is a way of being in control of his own life, despite the fears. As if we can save ourselves. Newman calls this pride and prays that God will forgive – *remember not past years*.

I know the desire for independence is a natural human tendency. How often have I said: 'I'll be right, I can do it', even though I am struggling to look after myself and do need another's care. I resist being dependent. Indeed, I haven't always prayed for God to lead me, as Newman says. When Paul recognised his resistance to God's invitation, his response was: 'who will rescue me... thanks be to God, through Jesus Christ Our Lord' (Romans 7:25).

But then, almost as if there has been some conversion, Newman's third verse recognises that, in fact, God has never let him down:

> *So long thy power hath blessed me, sure it still*
> *will lead me on*
> *O'er moor and fen, o'er crag and torrent till*
> *the night is gone*
> *And with the morn, those angel faces smile*
> *which I have loved long since, but lost a while*

This third verse has become a regular prayer for me. I have no doubt that *So long thy power hath blessed me* – a conviction that immediately prompts trust: *Sure it still will lead me on*. The prayer captures a basic truth of my faith that I am totally dependent on God's care. My every breath is God's breath, utter gift. In some sense, it is a fairly permanent state to be *far from home* and to be in the dark, feeling our way. We may not always enjoy that, but it is the reality, a foundational truth of our existence: God is the giver, we are the receivers, the underpinning of *Grace and Gratitude*. We have every reason to trust.

I am ever grateful to Cardinal Newman: his poem helped me to touch the deeper place in myself that enables me to persevere through the times of doubt and questioning, the times when I seem alone, not understood, not appreciated. In this deeper place, I slowly come to see that I have questions, but God has answers, I feel alone, but I am not alone. I rediscover trust, life, yes even gratitude.

Surely, this is true for all of us. Whatever of the crags and torrents in our life, we have all been well cared for and well blessed in our lives. I suggest that our deepening acknowledgment of that is best helped by the prayer that focuses on God's daily gift to us, keeping alive our memory of all the times God has gifted us.

> *So long thy power hath blessed me – sure it still will lead me on.*

Again, I say thankyou.

Epilogue

Gratitude is the memory of the heart.
Mary MacKillop

Gratitude is the only thing we can offer to God. God is the giver, we are the receivers. Our part is to receive. Interestingly, the very same words are used by St John of the Cross for his definition of contemplation: *Contemplation is to receive*. Though John speaks primarily of contemplative prayer, I tend to speak of a contemplative way of life – where the same definition applies, where we are daily dependent of God's gift of life.

To live contemplatively suggests a life lived at a slower, reflective pace, attentive and present to the moment, being fully present to whoever I am with, wherever I am and whatever I am doing, open to new awareness, ultimately open to God's gift in our everyday. I notice that, when I am more present to where I am and what I am doing, an offshoot is that I seem to enjoy what I am doing all the more. Another gift from God for which I am ever grateful.

We live in gratitude. Not unlike 'being in love', we live in gratitude. Gratitude permeates our life, not necessarily in our awareness, but often and spontaneously expressing itself in joyful thankyous. Grace and Gratitude.

www.ingramcontent.com/pod-product-compliance
Lightning Source LLC
Chambersburg PA
CBHW011954090526
44591CB00020B/2766